# A

## Aircraft Carrier

# B

## Balboa Park

# C

**Coronado Beach**

# D

## Del Mar

# E

# Embarcadero

# F

**Fish Tacos**

# G

## Gaslamp Quarter

# H

## Harbor Island

# I

## Imperial Beach

# J

## Julian

# K

# Kayaking

# L

La Jolla Cove

Mission Bay

**N**

**North Park**

# O

## Old Town

# P

**Petco Park**

# Q

**Quail Botanical Gardens**

# R

Ramona

# S

## SeaWorld

**Torrey Pines**

# V

# Valley Center

# W

## Whale Watching

X

**X-treme Sports**

# Y

# Yacht

# Z

## Zoo Safari Park

## Now It's Your Turn!

*Which San Diego attraction would you like to visit the most and why?*

Can you draw your favorite animal from the San Diego Zoo illustration and explain what you find fascinating about it?

Imagine you are on a yacht in San Diego Bay. What do you see around you, and what would you like to do?

Made in the USA
Las Vegas, NV
18 December 2024

14945626R00017